Leadership At Its Strongest

What Successful Managing Partners Do

By
Robert J. Lees
August J. Aquila
Derek Klyhn

Copyright © 2013 Robert J. Lees, August J. Aquila, and Derek Klyhn. All rights reserved. Printed in the United States of America. No part of this publication may be reproduced or transmitted in any form or by any means, electronic or mechanical, including photocopying, recording or use of any information storage or retrieval system, for any purpose without the written permission of Robert J. Lees, or August J. Aquila, or Derek Klyhn. Any persons, companies, and organizations listed in examples and case studies herein are purely fictitious for teaching purposes, unless the example states otherwise. Any resemblance to existing organizations or persons is purely coincidental.

Published by
Bay Street Group LLC
PO Box 5139
East Hampton, N.Y. 11937 U.S.A.
www.baystreetgroup.com / (631) 604-1651

ISBN-13: 978-0982714751
ISBN-10: 0982714750

Advance Praise

"*Leadership At Its Strongest* is a powerful book. Rob Lees, August Aquila and Derek Klyhn have captured the essence of leadership. You won't be disappointed! A must-read for anyone who leads a firm or team."
– Richard Caturano,
Chairman, American Institute of Certified Public Accountants; Executive Managing Partner-Boston, McGladrey LLP

"You can read a 600-page tome from one of our profession's management gurus or you can read this slim volume of insight and wisdom. I recommend the second choice. Use the time savings to put this good advice to work in leading your firm."
– Bob Bunting,
Past CEO, Moss Adams, Chair International Services Group

"This is an excellent road map for being a successful managing partner. It touches on both the strategic as well as the soft-skill people issues, both of which are necessary to lead a professional services firm in this day and age. Many years of collective wisdom are captured in this short piece – A very worthwhile read!"
– Gordon Krater,
Firm Managing Partner, Plante & Moran, PLLC

Dedication

To the partners who participated in our research

and made this publication a reality

CONTENTS

LEADERSHIP AT ITS STRONGEST 9

1. THE MODEL 13

2. SETTING DIRECTION 17

      CHAPTER QUESTIONS 21

3. GAINING COMMITMENT 23

      CHAPTER QUESTIONS 30

4. EXECUTION 31

      CHAPTER QUESTIONS 36

5. PERSONAL EXAMPLE 37

      CHAPTER QUESTIONS 43

6. A FEW FINAL THOUGHTS 45

      CHAPTER QUESTIONS 47

APPENDIX 49

MANAGING PARTNER 360 FEEDBACK SURVEY 51

ABOUT THE AUTHORS 55

Leadership At Its Strongest: What Successful Managing Partners Do

Professional services is one of the most critical sectors in all Western economies and an increasingly important one in every other world economy. But, the usual measures of scale, like revenues, the number of firms or the number of professionals, don't adequately reflect the importance of the sector.

What makes professional services so critical is the influence professional firms have on their clients' activities. Whether the influence comes through strategic advice, legal opinion, transaction origination and support, tax minimization, or an audit opinion, every business is reliant, in some form, on the opinion of a professional services firm.

In addition, and at least as important given the move away from self-regulation, there is the critical regulatory role of the accountants and lawyers tasked with ensuring the probity of the world's financial markets. All of which makes the task of ensuring that each of the firms is a role model of its profession's expertise, values and ethics absolutely key.

When firms were relatively small, that wasn't a difficult task. However, as firms have increased in scale, geographic reach and service offerings, the task of running a professional services firm has become extremely complex. And that's without considering changing client expectations, increasing competition between firms, threats to the traditional business model from offshoring and the increasing number of virtual firms, the increasing number of Western economy-based firms operating in countries with social and business norms sometimes far removed from their own, the arrival of a generation with very different expectations than their predecessors, and calls for greater transparency and regulation in the light of the financial meltdown.

In our combined 50-year association with professional services firms, every one of the hundreds of firms we have worked with around the world has seen the number, scale and complexity of the challenges they face increase significantly.

Being a managing partner, never the easiest of roles, is now one of the most complex and challenging roles in any organization in any business sector anywhere in the world. And yet, every managing partner we know admitted that they took on the role without any real understanding of what it entailed and without being sure if they had the capabilities to do it effectively. They also described how the typical high need-for-achievement culture within professional services firms, with its intolerance of perceived failure, made it almost impossible for them to ask for help when they needed it and for their colleagues to offer it.

Given that the majority of our consulting time has been spent helping managing partners increase their effectiveness, we decided to add to our anecdotal knowledge and years of desk research by asking 150 practicing and managing partners in a cross section of accounting, consulting and law firms across Europe and the United States, what they believe successful managing partners do.

With most of the discussions referencing the performance of one or more managing partners, all of our discussions were naturally confidential. Consequently, unless we were given permission to use the examples or they are in the public domain, all of the examples we quote are anonymous.

The following model, which synthesizes all of the interviews and our many hundreds of interactions and discussions over the last 30 years, describes what managing partners need to do to deliver the sustained high performance that their partners, their clients and the markets want and expect.

It is the translation of these expectations into reality, which distinguishes the truly successful managing partners, and all of the partners involved in the research were clear that being a strong and effective leader is what differentiated the truly successful managing partners.

As leaders, they provided a clear sense of direction, a vision that reflected a stage on the journey and the strategies for achieving it; who got and sustained their partners' commitment for achieving the vision; who helped the partners and the firm's people deliver outstanding client service, and whose individual performance personified everything they wanted the firm to stand for.

And, of course, they created a culture of sustained high performance and profitability.

1. THE MODEL

Our model of what successful managing partners do is adapted from the leadership model in *When Professionals Have To Lead* (WPHTL), which Rob co-authored with Tom DeLong and Jack Gabarro.

We have used the same overarching dimensions of Direction, Commitment, Execution and Personal Example, but have modified the behaviours to identify what successful managing partners do. As we firmly believe that firm context should be a major influence on the choice of managing partner and what managing partners are tasked to do, we have also made Context an explicit variable, rather than the implicit one it is in *WPHTL*.

Our work shares the same underpinning as *WPHTL*: that professional services firms are different from their corporate counterparts in a number of ways, which impact their functioning and, therefore, their leadership.

Regardless of their ownership structure, most professional services firms either operate as partnerships or would prefer to operate as partnerships. The tensions between being a business and the loss of the values and ethics of being a partnership featured strongly in our discussions and are referred to in how managing partners gain and sustain their partners' commitment.

The compressed hierarchy and the loosely coupled nature of their organizations, which make relationships as critical

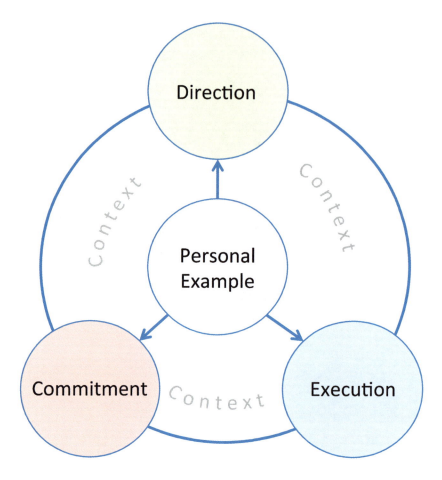

Adapted from the Leadership Model in When Professionals Have To Lead: A New Model For High Performance, Thomas J. Delong, John J. Gabarro, Robert J. Lees, Harvard Business School Press, 2007

© Robert J Lees, August J Aquila, Derek Klyhn, November 2011

internally as they are externally, are also significant influences, as are the people who work in them.

Professional services firms are full of high-need-for-achievement personalities, who join professional services firms to interpret the profession's body of knowledge and serve clients.

Most of them (and this is especially true of partners) consider anything remotely bureaucratic or administrative – in fact, anything that gets in the way of serving clients – as an absolute anathema.

Rarely, do they want to get involved in anything that smacks of management or leadership, preferring to leave that to others. But, and it's a big but, most partners do want their say in how things are done and, critically, in what the firm is trying to achieve. They believe they have a right to be heard and that their opinions should count.

Another factor, which can have an impact on the way firms function, and especially their managing partners, is that, in most firms, the managing partners are elected by their peers and operate with their goodwill. When managing partners are limited to two four-year terms, as they often are in Europe (but much less so in the United States), the re-election process, which usually starts after three years, can be an unwanted distraction from the real challenges the managing partners face.

So, how do successful managing partners respond to the internal and external challenges they face?

The first thing they do is set direction.

2. Setting Direction

Without exception, all of the partners we spoke to talked about the need to have a clear sense of direction that the partners, in particular, could coalesce around. But what they considered even more important is the translation of that direction into a compelling vision and the strategies for achieving it.

And compelling is the key word. If the vision isn't compelling, if it doesn't resonate with the partners, then their willingness to embrace the ideas and take action is greatly reduced, as, therefore, is the firm's momentum.

> **Direction**
>
> o Provide a compelling direction and strategy
>
> o Know where the firm "is" and what is possible
>
> o Focus people's attention and actions around key priorities
>
> o Constantly assess the firm's markets and determine when and how to respond
>
> o Share successes that clarify what the future looks like

Put simply, the partners must own the direction and strategies, as they are the people who will implement them. The managing partner has a major role to play in helping the partners sustain their enthusiasm and commitment, but, as we know, change only occurs where the work gets done.

The managing partner of one of the firms we talked to

explained how he had come back from Harvard Business School's Leading Professional Service Firms program with renewed energy and a determination to drive the firm forward. So, he outlined his vision of moving the firm from its regional base to becoming a leading national firm to his partners and talked about what they needed to do to get there. But, to his abject disappointment, nothing happened.

To the partners, the vision was just too aspirational, achievable only through a merger, which they felt they would be on the wrong side of. Concerned about the lack of action, the managing partner visited all of the offices to talk through the plans and, during these visits, the partners' concerns surfaced. Recognising his mistake, the managing partner reset the vision and started the journey again, helped this time by a specially selected group of influential partners.

But the managing partner quickly found the support and momentum he needed with a clearer description of what it meant in practice. He showed how they would significantly enhance their success in all of their markets if they endeavoured to be the best at everything they did. And they would be on the right side of any merger, if they decided to go down that route.

One critical thing the managing partner did was to concentrate on a small number of key priorities. That continuous focus ensured people's energy wasn't dissipated across too many initiatives, a lot of which the managing partner felt wouldn't yield the behaviour change he was looking for. This time, the firm made rapid steps forward and, by focusing their attention on how to improve, they quickly gained industry recognition for their outstanding client service.

In our discussion, the managing partner reflected how one of his mistakes had been getting too far in front of his partners, and the need to know where the firm "is" and what's possible (and, critically, what's not) was identified by managing and practicing partners alike as one of the things that truly successful managing partners always knew. One of the partners we spoke to put it succinctly, "Great managing partners have great antennae; they just seem to know what the mood is and how to get their partners on board. It's like they have a sixth sense."

But that sixth sense doesn't come by itself. It comes from being accessible and making sure you find out what the partners are thinking. All of the managing partners said it took time, but they all said it was worth it – as did the practicing partners, who felt their views were important and that they could influence what the firm was doing.

Despite the difficulty of scale, the managing partners of the large international firms recognized the importance of keeping close to their partners. It was inevitably a lot harder to do, but all of them had mechanisms in place to make sure that their partners could get their opinions known.

Understanding markets and knowing when and how to respond was also identified as a key factor in a managing partner's success.

When Nick Land took over as managing partner of Ernst &

Young's United Kingdom firm, he knew that continuing to do what the firm had done before was not the answer. At the time, he wasn't certain what was.

But it rapidly became evident that moving to industry sectors and co-locating the professionals from the different service lines was what the firm needed to do to improve performance. None of Ernst & Young's competitors were organized by industry sector and the move stole a march on the firm's competitors and led to a major uplift in revenues and profitability. What was really important in the move was that the arguments in favour of, essentially, turning the firm on its head, became compellingly self-evident. Everyone knew it was the "right" answer and lined up behind it.

In both of these examples and all of the others we heard about, one of the other things the managing partners did to engage the partners was to keep reinforcing the vision by sharing stories of the things that were working or had worked. The stories were also shared rapidly across the firm to help clarify what people would be doing in the future and that the direction the firm was travelling was the correct one and it was worth fighting for.

This clarification of what the future looks like in detail has the additional benefit of enhancing the partners' commitment to the direction and the vision and the strategies for getting there. Every partner told us a clear and detailed vision of the future is a crucial part of a successful managing partner's armoury.

CHAPTER QUESTIONS

1. As the managing partner have you created a compelling direction that your partners are committed to?

2. Are you realistic about what the firm can do and can't do?

3. How do you keep your partners engaged in the future of the firm?

4. Have you been successful in the translation of the firm's direction into a compelling vision and the strategies for achieving it?

5. Do you share what works well across the firm?

6. Are your priorities the right ones? Do they tie together?

3. Gaining Commitment

In our work with managing partners, we always talk about the importance of the partners "walking together," of sharing that common vision.

But if the partners are to share the vision, they have to play an active part in determining the firm's direction – and, critically, how it's going to get there.

In most firms, and particularly those with multiple locations, the partners typically give their proxy to the managing partner and the executive team to come up with the options they believe face the firm in its drive for sustained high performance.

Commitment
o Take the partners with them
o Motivate, empower and trust their partners
o Keep repeating the message
o Balance being a business and a profession
o Focus on the people who want to go with them rather than the people who don't

In the very best firms, the partners debate the options and, while it is incredibly rare for every partner to agree with every single aspect of the vision and strategy, the partners agree to line up behind the ultimate decisions.

There are no destructive conversations at the coffee machine or water cooler where some of the partners question the wisdom of the chosen actions. Conversations are inevitably overheard by the firm's people and disseminated throughout the firm at speed, ensuring that everyone is aware of the disagreements between the partners.

Unsurprisingly, this disunity within the partner ranks can significantly damage the firm's ability to achieve concerted momentum.

While scale makes engaging all the partners extremely difficult, it doesn't make it impossible. Smart managing partners find ways to engage the partners in one-to-ones and small groups and keep the debate alive so that everyone has the chance to share their views. The point about engagement, about taking the partners with you, came up in every single one of our discussions and its importance should not be underestimated.

We all know that simply voting in partner meetings typically ensures that the silent majority in the middle won't voice their opinions either way. It may be much more difficult to ensure every partner's voice is heard, but it is critical if the partners are going to play their part in moving the firm forward.

But engaging the partners and keeping them committed takes more than involving them in the decision-making process. Successful managing partners understand that there are levels of commitment and that the only way to get real and sustained commitment is through creating a culture of trust and empowerment, underpinned by a shared belief in what are now sometimes considered the old-fashioned values of partnership.

Without doubt, the most emotive element of all of our discussions was the loss of the values of partnership. Nearly every practicing partner spoke passionately about the loss of partnership values as their firms' leaders responded to the competitive challenges they faced by adding more bureaucracy (inevitable, to an extent, as scale increases) and running the firm as a business in which the only measures of success were individual billings and profit per equity partner.

It is a loss that we also keep coming across in our consulting work. A senior partner in one of the Big Four accounting firms summed up all of our discussions when he described how, if partners don't think about their legacy, about leaving something better for those who follow, rather than just their own tenure, you end up with a group of mercenaries who are in it for the money, who have no interest in their fellow partners or the firm, and whose natural instinct is to think of themselves first.

Successful managing partners balance the need to be a business with the values of partnership. They manage the delicate balancing act of being corporate at the top and practice-based below. It isn't easy but nor is it impossible.

The trick is to understand when moving away from being practice-based will result in increased operational efficiencies. But trust has to be at the core of any moves.

We mentioned earlier that professionals loathe anything

bureaucratic. But we know of many firms who ask their partners to account, in detail, for every minute of their time. To ask high-need-for-achievement professionals at the top of their field to provide what, to them, is bureaucratic data immediately implies a complete lack of trust and respect for their expertise and their position. It is simply a motivational disaster, which distances the partners from the firm. Partners know that they have to account for their time but we know too many firms that, often at the behest of the finance function, ask for a level of specificity that drives the partners to distraction.

The really smart managing partners have figured this out, and do everything they can to consolidate the link between their partners and the firm. They know what motivates their partners and, using the great antennae we referred to earlier, they stay tuned in to the mood of the partnership and know when to tack and when to stay on the same course. It's an exercise in sound judgement, which successful managing partners demonstrate in abundance.

Another piece of sound judgement is reflected in the way successful managing partners know that they have to be both visible and accessible – and, critically, when they need to increase their visibility.

In one of the firms we spoke to, there was a significant disagreement between the managing partner and his colleagues about the managing partner's visibility. Believing that he had put the firm on the right track, the managing partner decided to manage the majority of his communications through his practice leaders.

The problem was that the practicing partners we spoke to firmly believed that the move was a mistake. They wanted the managing partner to be visible, to be out, talking to the partners about the firm and how they were going to deal with the issues they faced. This need for visibility was exacerbated by the downturn in revenues the firm experienced immediately after the financial crisis and the uncertainty that it generated.

In this instance, the managing partner failed to respond to his partners' needs. This isn't the only example we have of managing partners failing to adjust their plans in the light of changing circumstances. But, the message is clear: to take your partners with you, you have to judge the mood of the partnership and respond accordingly. That does not mean always changing your stance, but it does mean explaining the reasons behind your decisions and, when necessary, gathering support for them.

The previous example also highlights another of the realities of dealing with high-need-for-achievement personalities – that, for all of their intelligence, they often lack a degree of self-confidence and need to keep being told they are doing the right thing.

In the Ernst & Young example we referred to earlier, Nick Land worked the need to change into all of his interactions with his partners. There were times when Nick wondered if the partners would ever "get it" but he, and lots of the managing partners we heard about, kept repeating their message to help reduce any uncertainty their partners had about the firm's direction and what it meant.

Constantly repeating the message is time consuming and at times deeply frustrating, but it is key to sustaining commitment. As is focusing on the people who want to go with you rather than those who don't.

In the process of collecting feedback on the model, we asked which of the behaviours particularly resonated, and this was one. Given our belief in the partners walking together, it's easy to believe that the focus should be on getting everyone in the same place. It's an easy mistake to make, but it is a mistake.

As we previously mentioned, not every partner will agree with every decision and, when momentum is key, the best way to achieve and maintain it is to engage the people who are enthusiastic, who want to be a part of what you are trying to achieve.

One of the other benefits of focusing on the partners who want to go with you is creating and expanding a group of influential partners, who can influence other people's behaviour.

In our earlier example of the managing partner who recalibrated his vision, one of the clear differences between his first and second attempts was the support he received from the group of influential partners he asked to help him. When you have smart people who want to be involved, leaving them on the sideline is a major tactical error.

Gaining commitment to the firm's direction and way of getting there is vital to ensuring success, but success ultimately hinges on what people actually do.

Professional services is an execution game. And with differentiation in professional services only achieved through delivery (both what you deliver and how you deliver it), the challenge for all firms is to ensure everything they do is aligned to ensuring the successful execution of everything they want to achieve.

CHAPTER QUESTIONS

1. How effective are you at gaining the commitment of your partners?

2. Do you focus on those partners who want to go with you or try to convert those who don't?

3. What do you do to increase the trust level in the firm?

4. Communication with the partner group is paramount. How do you normally communicate with your group? How can you do it better?

4. Execution

Momentum is critical in driving change, so it is no surprise that the initiation of activities that drive and support the strategy is key.

It is also one of the reasons why focus is critical. And yet one of the mistakes we see, more so in law firms than accounting or consulting firms, are initiatives having too much time between them.

Time, which enables people's attention to revert to "the day job," to the thing professionals like to do best of all – serve clients. And while client service must never be compromised, managing partners must not let their partners' attention be diverted from also implementing the strategies supporting the agreed direction.

> **Execution**
>
> o Initiate activities that drive and support the strategy
>
> o Appoint people who help them get things done
>
> o Help the partners be effective leaders
>
> o Help clients and the firm's people exceed their expectations
>
> o Stay on top of the firm's finances

Partners find it all too easy to revert to client work (it's what they are good at as well as what they like doing), and successful managing partners recognize this reality and keep their partners' heads up with a combination of focussed activities, the incessant repetition of the message, and by rapidly sharing successes across the firm.

Appointing people who can help them get things done is another key part of any managing partners' armoury. Managing partners must appoint people who they trust and who have the capabilities to help them implement their plans.

But capabilities, on their own, aren't enough. The people the managing partner chooses are his ambassadors, his representatives on a day-to-day basis and they must operate as leaders in their own right, influencing the partners and helping them play a positive part in shaping the firm's future.

Our final point about appointments is that choosing the right professional management group is as important as choosing the right partners. One of the consistent themes to emerge from our interviews was that the performance of the professional managers (finance, business development, human resources, talent management and marketing) has a direct impact on the partners' perception of their managing partner's performance.

With the appointments of the professional managers being the managing partner's specific responsibility, the partners used this group's performance as a major indicator of the managing partner's judgement and intentions. Many practicing partners cited the need for greater clarity around what the professional managers were trying to do and told us that, in the absence of this understanding, the partners used their own arbitrary criteria to evaluate the professional managers' performance – and, by association, an element of the managing partner's.

Knowing what "good" is when it comes to the professional management functions is another of the things that differentiates successful managing partners. They recognize that it isn't good enough to have someone who is an expert in their function; the critical element of the individual's performance is their ability to use their expertise to influence the partners' actions in a way that enhances the firm's performance.

Every firm we know understands the need to deliver outstanding client service. However, not all firms make the direct connection between outstanding client service and having the development processes in place that enable their people to deliver the necessary level of service.

The best firms do, but we know too many firms that do not invest the same attention on their own people as they do their clients.

And yet the link between satisfied, committed people and quality of work is inexorable. Helping the firm's people exceed their expectations is just as important as helping clients exceed theirs. And with differentiation through delivery, a firm's ability to make its professionals engagement ready faster and more effectively than its competitors is a clear source of competitive advantage – and, critically, economic advantage.

The importance of this dual focus is well understood by successful managing partners. They make sure that their firms have effective development processes, which enhance their professionals' "speed to experience."

They focus particularly on where most learning takes place – on the job. They ensure that the firm's partners are good coaches, who see developing their people as much a part of their job as serving their clients. They also ensure the firm's assignment allocation criteria include the development needs of the professionals and the interim and post-assignment discussions on whether the development needs are being addressed.

Investing in talent should be a "no-brainer;" sadly, for too many firms it isn't.

Being a good coach is just one of the expectations firms must have of their partners. In *When Professionals Have To Lead*, Rob and his colleagues Tom De Long and Jack Gabarro, explained why partners in today's firms have to lead. And, while most of the partners we know understand and accept that need, not everyone does, and not everyone understands what being an effective leader means.

In our discussions, every practicing and managing partner remarked that successful managing partners invested their time and energy in helping their partners become effective leaders. There was clarity about what being an effective leader meant and the firm provided the necessary development experiences when they were needed.

The successful managing partners understood the simple truth – that the partners are the culture in a professional services firm; what they do and how they do it determines how the firm's professionals behave. As one managing partner put it: "The partners have got to be leaders. If that takes up a lot of my time, in my opinion that's time well spent."

Every managing and practicing partner we spoke to mentioned that successful managing partners stay on top of the firm's finances. That didn't actually mean running the numbers themselves, which is what the managing partner of one law firm opted to do. While dispensing with the services of the finance director clearly saved the firm money, none of the practicing partners felt the move was a sound one – especially as it inevitably diverted the managing partner away from the leadership role the partners felt he should have been concentrating on.

To the partners, the managing partner's judgement was awry and, critically, he had failed to set the right example of what was important.

CHAPTER QUESTIONS

1. What do you do to help your partners become effective leaders? Do you devote enough time to doing this?

2. What activities do you start that drive and support the firm's strategies?

3. How effective is your management team in helping you get things done?

4. Have you appointed people who can really help you get things done?

5. Personal Example

Not every firm can be the market leader.

But every firm can have a culture of excellence, of striving to be the best at everything they do and of reinventing themselves as the markets for both clients and people change.

Professionals – people with a high-need-for-achievement – like to work in the firms they believe are the best, doing really stimulating work on the best clients and working with colleagues they see as their intellectual equals.

And with the inexorable link between people and clients, sustaining the supply of talented people needs an absolute commitment to doing everything to the best possible standard, which, of course, means being clear about what the "best" is now and, critically, what it's likely to be in the future.

> **Personal Example**
>
> o   Demonstrate an unswerving commitment to being the best
>
> o   Seek and listen to the opinions of others but know when it's time to act
>
> o   Reinforce the need for sustained high performance through their own actions
>
> o   Stay close to their/the firm's key client relationships
>
> o   Avoid the minutiae of management
>
> o   Make the tough people decisions
>
> o   Ask for help when they need it

Using their network to keep abreast of trends and new ideas and importing them into their firms is another thing that successful managing partners do well. They beg, borrow, or steal from anyone and anywhere to keep their firms up-to-date and, whenever possible, in front of their competitors.

The issue of reinvention and, particularly, the suitability of the current leadership model in the future, came up in our discussions with many of the partners in the Big Four accounting firms and the large international law firms. Expressing concern about their firms' difficulty in embracing diversity, the partners questioned how long it would be possible to continue with the "we know best" approach implicit the United States or United Kingdom colonization models.

Although the people responsible for the current process are often the very ones who need to break with tradition and take risks with people not from their own culture, the partners we spoke to were hopeful that their leaders would rise to the challenge. The partners accepted that the break with tradition would not be easy, but they firmly believed that success on a truly global scale was only sustainable by engaging difference and being prepared to accept that there isn't just one way of doing things (i.e., "ours") and that there are many different ways of achieving the same objective.

Continually seeking the opinions of others is important, but the key is knowing when to stop and act. It's another application of judgement that successful managing partners have in abundance.

They understand the causal link between delay and the dissipation of energy, and don't let things drag to the point where the loss of energy and commitment will result in the firm's ability to deliver its strategy being compromised. The ability to take the firm's temperature, to know where the partners "are" and to act accordingly is a core skill that feeds into many of the judgements that successful managing partners make.

We've referred to judgement several times and another significant application exhibited by successful managing partners is in their decision to stay close to their own and the firm's key client relationships.

We defined "close" in the research as not doing fee-earning work but being more than the review partner. "Close" was having serious conversations with key clients about their issues, about what was going on in their markets and being the "go to" person when informed comment was required by external agencies.

Given that success with clients is usually one of the key factors in a managing partner's election, most people would think that every managing partner would do this automatically. But, they would be wrong.

We met several managing partners who told us that the job of managing partner was too complex to enable them to continue to stay close to clients other than in an informal way.

This surprised us and left us concerned about how the

managing partners in question saw their role and also whether they were making the best use of their teams, particularly their professional managers.

Certainly, the managing partners deemed to be successful by their practicing colleagues, all stayed close to their own and the firm's key client relationships. They all recognized the loss of credibility that would stem from not doing so, as well as the potential loss of "touch," of knowing what was going on in the firm around one of the firm's two main activities.

Asking the partners to sustain high levels of performance, including embracing different ways of doing things is impossible if you don't do it yourself and so being a role model, an exemplar of high performance, is an absolute prerequisite for all successful managing partners.

One of the things that great role models do is avoid the minutiae of management. Without exception, the practicing partners wanted their managing partner to be an effective leader – a leader who did all of the things we have described; and who carried them out in an authentic manner; with honesty and integrity and with a clear understanding of who they were, what they were good at and, critically, what they weren't. They wanted a leader who earned their respect not just for what they did but also for the way they did it.

What the partners absolutely didn't want was their managing partner to disappear into the minutiae and cease to be visible except for messages about time recording, bill collection or some other administrative detail.

It wasn't that the partners believed the detail was unimportant; they just saw it as the professional managers' job not the managing partner's. The partners did recognize that there would be times when the managing partner would have to get involved in administrative issues that absorbed a lot of time and effort, but they wanted that to be the exception not the rule.

One of the things that managing partners didn't always do, but their practicing partners thought they should do, was to take the tough people decisions. As it was frequently put to us, "we all know who the underperformers are and it's the impact on the rest of the partners of them not being dealt with that's the problem."

This sentiment was expressed in a slightly different way at the close of many of our interviews, when, having listened to a story of an outstanding managing partner in action, we asked if there was anything they could have done to be even more effective. In every case, "take the tough people decisions" was the first or second response.

We all know that dealing with underperforming partners or partners who don't want to embrace changing needs is a difficult and complex task. But in every instance the partners wanted their managing partner to deal with them – to deal with them in accordance with the partnership's values, and to deal with them rather than ignore them.

We have made "Ask for help" the final behaviour in the model. It is where we started – helping managing partners to make sense of their role.

Despite the classic professional services firm phenomena of managing partners not being able to ask for help and their partners not providing any, despite knowing some would be welcome, we have noticed that successful managing partners typically ignore convention and ask for help when they need it.

We don't know anyone (most certainly not ourselves) who is good at everything and gets everything right all of the time. Smart managing partners recognize this reality and have the self-confidence to ask for help when they need it.

Getting to a position where asking for help, and receiving it, may still be a challenge in a lot of firms. But it's a challenge worth taking on and winning because winning demonstrates that the managing partner has truly changed the firm's culture and that their leadership has made a positive difference to what the firm does.

And making a positive difference is what every managing partner we know aspires to do.

CHAPTER QUESTIONS

1. When you need help, do you ask for it?

2. As the firm leader do you have an unswerving commitment to always do and be the best?

3. What do you do that keeps you close to the firm's key client relationships?

4. Do you make or avoid the tough people decisions?

6. A Few Final Thoughts

One of the things that there was universal agreement about was that the role of managing partner is just too important and too complex to leave the selection of the appropriate candidate to chance.

With the scale of the challenges firms are facing, no firm we know can afford not to identify and develop a group of partners with the ability to successfully take on the role of managing partner in the future.

We say "group of partners" as this is where context is absolutely critical. The right person to lead a major geographic, cross-cultural expansion isn't necessarily the right person to take tough decisions to correct reducing financial performance or to deal with significant changes in the firm's business model in response to changes in technology and low cost competition.

For firms, the key is to identify a number of potential managing partners and give them experience of operating in different contexts, which can then be used to determine who is most suited to the challenges the firm faces at the time of the managing partner's appointment and during their likely tenure.

Making the right call, choosing the right managing partner, is critical to every firm's future success. And what we know from our research and all of our work in professional firms is that successful managing partners are strong and effective leaders – leaders whose picture of the future excites and energizes the firm's partners and people, who help everyone, clients and colleagues, to exceed their expectations and whose personal performance personifies everything the firm stands for.

CHAPTER QUESTIONS

1. Do you currently receive structured feedback on your leadership from your team and colleagues?

2. Have you conducted an assessment of strengths and development areas for your executive team?

APPENDIX

MANAGING PARTNER 360 FEEDBACK SURVEY

If you liked what you just read and really want to become a more effective leader, we offer a range of services that can help you in your quest. We offer the first 360 leadership survey designed especially for managing partners of professional services firms. It differs from internal 360 surveys by focusing totally on the managing partner role, giving deep feedback on the essence of leadership in professional services firms.

The survey gives managing partners:

- Structured feedback on your leadership from your team and colleagues,
- An assessment of strengths and development areas for executive and management teams,
- A basis to develop managing partners, improve your impact and boost the performance of the firm,
- A structure for reflecting and talking about leadership in the professional services firm environment, and
- Support for succession planning, talent management and career transition planning for managing partner roles.

THE FOUNDATIONS OF THE SURVEY

The survey is based on research by Rob Lees, Derek Klyhn, and August Aquila. It describes what managing partners need to do to deliver the sustained high performance that their partners, clients and markets want and expect.

POTENTIAL USES

The 360 has many potential applications, including:

- o Managing partner developmental reviews
- o Supporting executive and management team development
- o Support succession planning
- o As an adjunct to leadership programs for aspiring and current managing partners
- o Support coaching and mentoring arrangements

FURTHER INFORMATION AND PRICING

Contact:

August Aquila in the United States: +1 952-930-1295 or aaquila@aquilaadvisors.com,

Liz Baltesz in the United Kingdom +44 (0)7778 738 296 or liz.baltesz@mollerpsfgcambridge.com, or

Derek Klyhn in the United Kingdom +44 (0)7901 515 188 or derek.klyhn@mollerpsfgcambridge.com.

ABOUT THE AUTHORS

Rob Lees is a founding partner of Møller PSFGroup and consultant to professional services firm leaders worldwide. He is also co-author of the best-selling *When Professionals Have To Lead*. For more information, see www.mollerpsfgcambridge.com.

August Aquila is an internationally known speaker, writer, and consultant to professional services firms. He is CEO of Aquila Global Advisors. He is also the co-author of *Performance is Everything; Compensation as a Strategic Asset;* and *Client at the Core*. He can be reached at 1-952-930-1295 or aaquila@aquilaadvisors.com. For information see, www.aquilaadvisors.com.

Derek Klyhn is a founding partner of Møller PSFGroup and consultant to professional services firm leaders and their teams. He can be reached at 07901 515188 or derek.klyhn@mollerpsfgcambridge.com. For more information, see www.mollerpsfgcambridge.com.

FROM THE PUBLISHER

Bay Street Group LLC is a leading global provider of actionable intelligence to the professional services fields.

Please visit **CPA Trendlines Research** for facts and figures, insights and implications for tax and accounting professionals and their firms, at cpatrendlines.com.

More resources, at baystreetgroup.com/store, include:

- Professional Services Marketing 3.0
- Trends in Accounting Firm Marketing Strategies
- How to Increase Your Billing Rates
- How To Bring in New Partners
- Tax Season Opportunity Guide
- The Rosenberg MAP Survey
- CPA Firm Succession Planning
- How to Negotiate a CPA Firm Merger
- CPA Firm Management & Governance: The Essential Managing Partner's Guide to Running a CPA Firm Like a Business
- Strategic Planning and Goal Setting for Results
- What Really Makes CPA Firms Profitable
- Effective Partner Relations and Communications
- How to Operate a Compensation Committee
- The Guide to Planning the Firm Retreat

Also: The SevenKeys to Successful CPA Firm Management, at sevenkeyscpa.com

Made in the USA
Charleston, SC
22 March 2013